Daniel Richard Randall

Cooperation in Maryland and the South

Daniel Richard Randall

Cooperation in Maryland and the South

ISBN/EAN: 9783337005092

Printed in Europe, USA, Canada, Australia, Japan

Cover: Foto ©ninafisch / pixelio.de

More available books at **www.hansebooks.com**

JOHNS HOPKINS UNIVERSITY STUDIES

IN

HISTORICAL AND POLITICAL SCIENCE

HERBERT B. ADAMS, Editor

History is past Politics and Politics present History — *Freeman*

SIXTH SERIES

XI-XII

COÖPERATION

IN

MARYLAND AND THE SOUTH

By DANIEL R. RANDALL, Ph. D

BALTIMORE

PUBLICATION AGENCY OF THE JOHNS HOPKINS UNIVERSITY

1888

TABLE OF CONTENTS.

COÖPERATION IN MARYLAND AND THE SOUTH.

BY DANIEL R. RANDALL, PH. D.

The field which I have chosen to explore in this study of
·coöperation and coöperative methods, differs so materially
from those chosen by my co-laborers that I feel it necessary
to preface this paper with a few words of introduction.
Industrial life in the Southern states is unique in its
newness, claiming an existence of but two decades, and in
consequence is lacking in industrial experience. Strikes,
trades-unions, and coöperation are comparatively new ideas,
new issues, which the Southern laborer finds difficult to
grasp, from inexperience and a failure to appreciate their
value in labor economy. Maryland and Texas may claim to
be exceptions to the above. The former has enjoyed all the
benefits of a Northern education, industrially speaking, and
the latter, from its cosmopolitan origin, claims human contributions with human experience from every state in the
Union. The empire state of the South should, in truth,
because of this dissimilarity with her environment, be
treated separately.

The South lay largely in a state of stagnation, socially and
industrially, from colonial days until the outbreak of the
civil war, when the defense of political beliefs and principles
demanded the urgent and strenuous exertion of every citizen.
The lethargy, hereditary and universal, which had bur-
dened the Southern citizen from his birth, was in an
instant thrown aside, and his noble manhood first put
to the test, became quickly apparent. The war, with its
accompanying trials, suffering and horrors, was now his
bitter lot. The weakness which invariably follows the

489

struggle, from tired muscles and exhausted energy, has been the lot of the South since the close of that terrible conflict, yet the years of peace have witnessed returning strength upheld by increasing hope. The census of 1860 showed a population in the South of 8,000,000 freemen and 4,000,000 slaves. The following ten years witnessed a complete upheaval of existing conditions, and, the slave element disappearing, the census of 1870 returned 14,000,000 freemen.

There is a mine of thought and study in these figures. The two elements of industrial society, capital and labor, had been hitherto united in the person of the slave, a chattel in his master's hand. Four years of internecine strife, the loss of six billions in money, and nine hundred thousand lives, had torn these elements violently asunder, and the New South was born. The "irrepressible conflict" of labor and capital, waged in the Northern states since the days of the revolution, now first appears in the life of the South. She has herself experienced a revolution, fought, indeed, with the beasts at Ephesus. Her wealth has been thrown to the winds, and the chattel become an equal in the eyes of the law. Yet testimony proves that no section can claim a more prosperous laboring population than the South; none are in fuller sympathy with the employing and landowning class than these *quondam* chattels. The negro problem is seeking its own solution and cannot long remain a subject for economic discussion or legislative debate. "The new South presents a perfect democracy, the oligarchs leading in the popular movement;—a social system, compact and closely knitted, less splendid on the surface but stronger at the core. Ruffians have maltreated the negro, rascals misled him, philanthropists established a bank for him,"[1] yet he survives, better fitted by a schooling in adversity for the duties that citizenship imposes. Law and arms can enfranchise, grant liberty and equality, but to conscience

---

[1] Grady on the New South.

and common sense must be left the final victory of enlighten-
ment and progress over ignorance, depravity and supersti-
tion.

Twenty years have passed since this industrial revolution
of the South, years of rapid development, yet industrial
society there is still in its youth, and many years more
are needed before she can claim an equal maturity with
her Northern sisters.

The South is still in the agricultural stage of society,
though evolution toward the commercial is most marked.
Georgia and Alabama stand out as prominent examples of
this development.

The marked absence of the many causes leading to
labor combination and industrial reform, has greatly nar-
rowed the scope of the present inquiry. My study of the
subject of coöperation has consequently been confined
chiefly to the states of Maryland and Texas, where industries
have developed and where industrial life has exhibited
similar characteristics to those in the Northern and Western
states.

Pure coöperation, with its slight taste of philanthropy,
implying a division of net profit between stockholders and
patrons of the enterprise; in other words, the Rochdale
system, has rarely, to my knowledge been practiced, and
rarely attempted in Maryland and the South, except among
the Patrons of Husbandry. Many coöperative enterprises
have started with the Rochdale system as one of their principles, but a lack of profit or of resolution has destroyed
their good intention. Where this principle is not adhered
to the coöperative method becomes identical with the joint-
stock company. About thirty productive establishments,
claiming to be coöperative, have fallen within my province,
twenty of which are in the four states of Maryland, Virginia,
West Virginia and Texas. Some of these exist at present
only in the minds of certain enthusiasts who correspond
with labor papers, and many more live but to be christened.
I have taken in each chapter examples of living industries

and establishments whose permanency can hardly be questioned. Owing to the fact that so many of the coöperative enterprises are in their experimental stage, or have just passed their first year without mishap, I have been often unable to gain information about them from their managers.

I.

PRODUCTIVE COÖPERATION.

Productive coöperation in the South claims an age of but fifteen years and the state of Maryland as its birthplace. It had its incipiency in the period immediately following the Paris Commune of 1871, when the organization of the Internationalists had many votaries in the South. The great social agitation of the period went forth from Paris as a center as do the ripples in water from a central point of disturbance. This was an epoch in communistic enterprise when the theories of Cabet and Saint-Simon were being put to practical test in the Western states. A free society, based upon coöperative organization of production, was the ultimate aim. The party of the Internationalists in Maryland determined to inaugurate coöperative production by establishing a coöperative shoe factory in Baltimore. Under the management of Samuel A. Pierce, perhaps their most active member, the factory started in 1871, a joint-stock company with one hundred members. Profits were to be equally divided between capital and labor, stockholder and employé. The enterprise had a lingering existence of three years and then failed through treachery among the stockholders in disposing of their shares. Competition, too, with machine-made goods was found to be ruinous, but Pierce and a few others remained undaunted.

A year or more after the failure of the first, a second shoe factory was started in humble fashion with six members, and these all practical workers in the enterprise. The capital was small, entirely owned by the workers. Enterprise number two lasted but one year, when five members sold out to the sixth, and the first stage in productive coöperation was passed. For several years coöperative enterprise lay dormant, dispirited by the failure of early attempts. But it again revived in 1884, when a coöperative bakery was established in Baltimore. A company was formed and stock issued, two hundred shares at five dollars. With the \$300 of paid capital the company purchased the good will and fixtures of an unsuccessful baker on Cross street, and with the patronage of the labor organizations, with their membership of fourteen thousand promised, the coöperative bakery opened September 15, 1884. A year's trial was enough to convince even the most sanguine of the forty members that a little shop employing but three men and no machinery was powerless before the large steam bakeries of the city. The promised patronage of the toiling masses went for naught, and the patrons of the former bakery withdrew, styling the new enterprise a humbug. The shop was resold to its former owner, and, save a recollection of money lost, nothing remained of this enterprise. But it had sown good seed, and the year 1886 witnessed a revival of the same idea. A coöperative bakery with two hundred and fifty stockholders has been started, and, though at present in the toils, it is hoped that the patronage of the workingmen will place it on a good footing. The year 1884 was marked by a general revival throughout the land in coöperative methods, stimulated by the power and activity of the labor organizations, and especially by that of the Knights of Labor.

By this order the Kentucky Railroad Tobacco Company, at Covington, was incorporated September 1, 1884. The capital of this enterprise now amounts to \$20,000, divided into 2,000 shares, which are held only by the employés of the factory. The stock is of two classes, capital stock and wage-producing stock, each receiving equally of the dividends issued out of the net profits of the company. By the laws of the company the employés are paid weekly wages in cash equal to that received by laborers in neighboring factories. Wages are considered six per cent. upon wage-producing stock of employés, and capital stock also receives its six per cent. interest.

The number of employés and stockholders now amounts to thirty-five, and their annual production is estimated at about $150,000. Every worker in the factory is required to be a Knight of Labor, yet in spite of this a rival coöperative tobacco company seems to have obtained the exclusive recognition of the National Convention of the Knights of Labor. This is the National Knights of Labor Coöperative Tobacco Company, of Raleigh, N. C., incorporated January 1, 1886, with an authorized capital of $10,000. It has many laws like those of the last mentioned company without its novel and perhaps misunderstood system of profit-sharing. The stock is exclusively held by Knights of Labor or their assemblies, no assembly or individual being allowed to hold more than fifty shares or $125 worth, and no shareholder is entitled to more than one vote. The coöperative principle of this company may be gathered from section 25 of their rules and regulations: "The net profits of all business carried on by this company, after paying for or providing for the expenses of management, interest on loan-capital, and paying eight per cent. on paid-up shares of capital, shall be divided into three equal parts, viz.: One to labor, one to capital, and one to the coöperative fund of the Knights of Labor." The company may also create a reserve fund to meet contingent expenses and losses. The business of the company must be deemed highly satisfactory, though the showing for the ten months ending January 1, was not as favorable as for the first three or six months of the enterprise. This is due largely to the apathy of members and their patrons toward the concern after the excitement of the start had subsided, and the causes which compelled its formation were forgotten. The sales for the last year amounted to about $7,000, and, after the payment of all expenses, the stockholders realized a profit of ten per cent. upon the paid-in stock, amounting now to $3,660. Prospects are improving, and there is every indication that the present will be a fortunate

.year. The disposition among the working classes to start coöperative business is marked, but the indisposition to maintain them after a beginning has been affected is also as clearly marked.

Productive coöperation had one of its most hopeful examples in the glass manufacturing company, started at Baltimore in 1885. It originated in a general strike of blowers in the glass-works of the city. The strike, as a whole, was unsuccessful, but a few among the employés determined to stick to their principles and start a rival factory rather than return under the old conditions. A piece of land was given them by a friend at Mt. Winans, a station on the Baltimore and Ohio Railroad, about five miles from the city limits. Here the glass-works were constructed. Capital stock was issued at first to the amount of $10,000, at one hundred dollars a share, but finding this too small, it was later increased to $25,000 and again to $40,000.

Of this but $18,000 has been actually paid in, and is largely owned by the directors, though some little by the other employés. The management was very democratic, being in the hands of a board of twenty-three, all of them skilled workmen, out of which a president, treasurer and secretary-agent were chosen yearly. No shareholder could own more than five shares, though some of the stock had been disposed of before this became a law. The works can employ one hundred men and boys when worked at their greatest capacity, and produce five hundred gross of bottles a week. Nominally this enterprise was founded and managed upon the Rochdale principle. The secretary wrote: "We have started the works in such manner as we claim none others have done in the history of these United States, our great impulse being to resist the iron despotism of capitalists."

The philanthropic and harmonious feeling in which the enterprise was undertaken may be readily seen in this article of their laws. "The profits are to be disposed of in the following manner: Six per cent. interest is to be paid upon the capital stock, and the balance subdivided, viz.: Five per cent. toward a contingent fund until fifty per cent. of the capital stock has thus accumulated; two and a half per cent. to be donated for educational purposes and the renting of a hall in which, by classes and lectures, the laborers are to be improved, and the surplus to be divided as a bonus to consumers and non-stockholding employés."

The Coöperative Glass Company is now considerably in debt, owing to changes in their plant, and the works have not been in active operation for a year. No dividends have, as yet, been declared, and likely will not be for several years. The long protracted and frequent strikes among glass-blowers during the past two years had tended greatly toward the betterment of this workingmen's enterprise, in which the matters of apprentices and union rates did not enter.

I have deferred until the last a description of perhaps the most flourishing enterprise in the South worked upon coöp-erative principles, though perhaps the youngest. This is the Furniture Workers' Coöperative Manufacturing Association of Baltimore. Like the majority of coöperative attempts in the South it is still in its infancy, yet has attained already such success that permanency seems secured. The eight-hour movement, which was to have taken effect May 1st, 1886, found among its advocates in Baltimore over three hundred joiners. For four weeks after the strike the proprietors of mills and furniture factories withstood the movement by closing their shops, and at the end of that time offered to take back those who would return under the old ten-hour system. A majority accepted the terms immediately, others held off until their ready money was exhausted and then succumbed, so that two months after the movement was inaugurated but twenty-five stood by the eight-hour demand.

These had been black-listed by their employers and were unable to obtain work in the city. This little body had not been idle meanwhile, but obtained from eighty-five of their brother joiners subscriptions amounting to $1,800 before

32

July 1st, a capital for the new coöperative enterprise. Machinery had to be purchased, buildings rented, and work well in progress before they could expect credit from firms or individuals. Many obstacles were in their path, and, added to all, the attempt of their former employers to hurt their business and reputation. This was seen in several instances. An agreement was made and signed with a large company to furnish the necessary machinery for the factory. After several unexplained delays the machine company finally repudiated its contract upon the untenable ground that the capital of the new enterprise was too small for them to succeed in business. Later investigation proved conclusively that their old employers were the direct cause of this breach of contract. Nothing daunted, the men purchased necessary machinery on favorable conditions from Clarkson & Co., of Baltimore, and a building, once used as a furniture factory, was refitted with improvements. Their old antagonists were again on their track, threatening to boycott those who furnished lumber and supplies, believing in the old-time remedy of suffocation in infancy rather than the doubtful rivalry of riper years. Work began at No. 1 Granby street, and the factory became crowded with finished ware. Two houses on East Baltimore street were rented and are now used as ware and show-rooms. On the 15th of January, 1888, the company occupied new and larger quarters on Preston and President streets. The factory is nearly five times the size of the Granby street house, and it is estimated that their second half-year will make an output twice that of the first six months. The force of workmen employed at the start was twenty-five, fifteen of whom were joiners, but the business of the association has so rapidly increased that about seventy-five men are now in constant occupation. The manager of the factory, elected by the stockholders, proved an unfortunate choice, but neither treachery within, nor conspiracy from without, has undermined a business founded upon grit and energy. On the first of January last an inventory of stock, fixtures and debts was made, and revealed to these unpretentious toilers, who could lay no claims to business ability, a state of affairs highly encouraging. Though expecting but living wages during the first year of their enterprise, they have, in truth, received but two-thirds of their wages, willing to endure some privations until they have attained their aims. These, in the words of one of the coöperators, are two in number, first, to show the employers of labor that coöperation among workers can succeed and friendly relations with one another be maintained; and secondly, that machinery, which makes slaves of their workmen, must become the slave of the workmen. The capital of the association is $50,000, at one hundred dollars a share. Shareholders must belong to the Furniture Workers' Trade Union, of Baltimore, or to their International Union, and can hold but one share of stock. All the employés of the factory are required to be shareholders, but are allowed to pay for their stock by installments. The management of the association is in the hands of nine directors, elected by the stockholders, and out of this body are annually chosen the president, vice-president, secretary and treasurer. All of these officers, except the vice-president, are bonded in the sum of five hundred dollars each. The factory started August 1st with a capital of $1,800, which has since been increased to $6,326. The cost-value of the machinery is $4,956, from which it may easily be seen that little remained to pay as wages until a good credit had been established. The annual statement, rendered in July, 1887, showed that, after meeting all liabilities, the company still had a surplus of one hundred and seventy-two dollars. The sales for the first year amounted to $32,000. The sales at present average $60,000, which will be increased by one-half after occupying their new quarters.

As nearly as can be estimated the assets on the first of January stood as follows :

Real estate, cost value	$25,000
Machinery and fixtures	4,956
Outstanding accounts	4,000
Merchandise inventory	10,000
	$43,956

The coöperators are zealous, determined men, and without doubt can make their business a successful one, though the present is a little early to expect great results.

The Knights of Labor Coöperative Soap Factory, of Richmond, is an enterprise, according to report, in prosperous circumstances. It was inaugurated about three years ago for the manufacture of Knights of Labor soap, and has had to face a powerful competition. The larger manufacturers have combined to drive their product from the market. As the colored people use a great amount of soap, in washing for *other* people, it was upon their feelings and purses that the larger companies worked. They issued cards to all the colored churches of Virginia, offering a certain percentage of all sales to the churches, and its effects have been to greatly lessen a business at one time deservedly large. Its present condition is unknown, as no replies have come to letters.

Glass-works at Annapolis have lately been reorganized upon a coöperative plan, and have taken the mantle of the Baltimore company upon their shoulders. The enterprise started two years ago as a joint-stock company, many of its members being of the laboring population. Finding it impossible to succeed through constant disagreement with the employés, the managers have adopted a coöperative plan by agreement with them. One-half of the laborers' wages are withheld until the end of the year, when, from the net balance, a six per cent. interest is first paid on the capital stock of $15,000, then the half-wages due the employés, and the remainder is divided between capital and labor. The inauguration has been too recent to judge of its success.

The same may be said of the coöperative shirt factory recently started in Baltimore. Its aim is to give employment to women at good wages in the manufacture of Knights of Labor shirts. The capital is $5,000, at five dollars par, and owned generally by members of the Knights of Labor, though there is a general interest in its success in all classes. Work was started in an humble fashion at 107

West Fayette street, and is being carried on there still. Five hands are employed, and the sales have not been very extensive. Competition with the steam-power factories is very severe, and a capital sufficient to place this enterprise upon a competing basis is much needed.

The following are some of the more successful coöperative enterprises recently started in the South:

1. Coöperative Mining and Manufacturing Company, of Hopkins county, Ky., incorporated May, 1886. Capital $50,000, at par five dollars, and can only be held by Knights of Labor.

2. Knights of Labor and Farmers' Alliance Coöperative Publishing Company, Fort Worth, Texas. Chartered December, 1886. Capital $25,000.

3. Knights of Labor Coöperative Laundry, Fort Worth, Texas.

4. Coöperative Underwear Factory, Richmond, Va., with a branch establishment at Manchester. Started December, 1886.

5. Knights of Labor Coöperative Broom Factory, Lynch- burg, Va. Started October, 1886.

6. Coöperative Match Factory, Woodstock, West Virginia. Started in 1886.

7. Ohio Valley Coöperative Pottery, Wheeling, West Virginia.

8. The *Journal* Publishing Company, Baltimore, Md. Started in 1882 and re-organized in November, 1886. Publishes a daily German paper. Capital $5,000, is owned entirely by the ten employés. Has a circulation of over 6,000.

9. Coöperative Cooperage Shop, Baltimore. Started in March, 1887.

10. Coöperative Mercantile Association, Danville, Va.,

11. Coöperative Mining Company, Salisbury, Ala.

12. Coöperative Mining Company, Louisville, Ky.

13. Coöperative Coal Mining Company, Earlington, Ky.

II.

DISTRIBUTIVE COÖPERATION.

Systems of distributive coöperation have had little existence in the South, except in the two states of Maryland and
Texas. No instances can be found before the war of a
union of consumers for the cheaper purchase of necessaries,
though this is the simplest form known.

Industrial life in slavery days did not permit any such
scheme on the broad plantation, and in the city the care
for the small things of life was deemed below the dignity of
a Southern citizen. It seems doubtful to me whether in
the United States distributive coöperation will ever succeed.
The prevalence of the evil credit system, the mixed nation-
alities of our citizens, and the excited, everlasting rush in
industrial life, tend to render our people impatient and in-
different to the results obtainable in such a scheme.

Only a slow-thinking, penny-counting, frugal and pains-
taking people can bring coöperation of any character to a
success. In the South generally, its growth and development have been closely associated with that of the order of
Patrons of Husbandry, commonly known as the Grangers.
Maryland may justly lay some claim to the foundation of
this order, in the fact that Washington is its birth-place.
The order was founded by seven government clerks in 1867,
and during its life of twenty years has experienced many
ups and downs. In the first ten years of its existence the
growth of the order in wealth and power was phenomenal,
but the following decade witnessed a loss of much of the
ground once gained. The labor agitations of the past
few years, the necessities for a better regulation of inter-
state commerce, and the growth of the railroad factor in
economic life have stimulated a recent increase in its
strength and interest. The reports of State Granges to the
National Grange are our chief source of information. Yet

these have to be used with caution, and suitable allowance has to be made for the high-flown enthusiasm of the masters. The reports for the last three years show a rather unsatisfactory condition in distributive coöperation among the Grangers in the South. The Rochdale system of competence to the purchaser, and the system of cash payments, are both suggested by the National Grange, and generally adopted. When failures occur, it is always claimed, they are due to a departure from these strict business principles and the laws of common sense. The Texas Coöperative Association has reaped the greatest success in this country in distributive coöperation. Chartered July 5, 1878, with an authorized capital of $100,000, but an actual capital of $250, this association is to-day the third largest receiver of cotton at the port of Galveston, and but for the action of the last Texas legislature, in prohibiting the chartering of local associations, this company would add the largest grocery business in the state to its credit. The stock of the association can be issued only to members of a Grange in good standing, individually or corporately. The paid-up capital now amounts to $51,715, the par value of stock being five dollars. One hundred and five coöperative associations have sprung into existence, scattered throughout the great state, and one hundred and fifty-five coöperative stores have grown from the seed planted but eight years ago. The central house of the association is at Galveston, with an agency in New York city, securing for patrons and others not belonging to the order the greatest advantages in the buying and selling of produce. The business of the Texas Coöperative Association for the year ending June 30, 1887, amounted to over $500,000, and the net profits of the year's work reach within a fraction of $20,000, to be distributed among the members of the order. By the constitution of the association profits are divided as follows: Shareholders are allowed ten per cent. on paid-up stock; a portion may be set aside by vote of the association to increase the capital, and the remainder is divided among stockholders and Patrons of

Husbandry not stockholders, the former receiving full and the latter half dividends. Profits derived from business furnished by Patrons not shareholders, and by non-Patrons, are styled an "accumulative fund," but are divided yearly among the shareholders. This class of business amounted last year to nearly $31,000, or about one-twentieth of the whole. This method then is not the pure form of coöperation, affording a competence to the purchaser, but is advantageous to Patrons of Husbandry alone.

The increase of capital and the amounts of the dividend fund, from the year 1879 until the present, are given in the following table:

Year.	Paid Capital.	Dividend Fund.	Stockholders.
1879	$ 250 00	....	...
1880	1,180 00	$ 1,385 00	...
1881	3,347 85	8,632 15	...
1882	14,000 00	12,654 73	...
1883	20,000 00	20,542 46	...
1884	27.500 00	17,349 49	...
1885	32,670 00	11,644 37	473
1886	39,730 00	19,694 41	497
1887	51,715 00	19,861 10	620

Each of the one hundred and fifty-five coöperative stores connected with the association does its own local business, and reaps its own profits. The total membership of the central and subordinate associations is now about six thousand. The total capital of the same is about $744,500. Total trade in the year 1885 in sales amounted to $1,977,579.90, from which was realized the total profit of $255,531.45. Failures among these subordinate associations do occur, but only, it is claimed, when the direct laws and injunctions of the association are departed from. Each association sends its representative to the yearly meeting and reports are then made and profits divided. Officers and seven of the thirteen directors of the association are elected at this August meeting. The latter choose the most important officer, the business manager. He gives a bond of $50,000, the secretary one of $3,000, and the treas-

urer one of $1,000, thereby greatly increasing the confidence
of the Grangers and other patrons. The *"Texas Farmer"*
is the organ of the State Grange, and is owned and published
weekly by the Patrons. It at present has a circulation
upward of four thousand. Another feature of the Texas
Coöperative Association is the Mutual Fire Insurance Company managed by the working force of the association. It
started operations September 15th, 1885, with no capital.
Its capital is now upward of $6,500, formed by the yearly
premiums of the insured. Patrons alone can be insured,
the Texas Coöperative Association guaranteeing the policies.
About $8,000 has been paid upon losses incurred by fire
since the organization of the company, and the amount
insured amounts to $136,030.98. Coöperation has done
wonders among the farmers throughout Texas. The societies have encouraged thrift, have been a means of education
and happiness among their members, and have engendered
the principles of practical economy. Under the vigorous
management of Mr. G. S. Rogers, who is and always has
been the business manager of the Texas Coöperative Association, coöperation and its sound principles will spread and
exert a potent influence among the citizens of that immense
state. The Farmers' Alliance, an association akin to the
Patrons, practices a form of coöperation in buying and selling
by contract with certain merchants. Its members are also
favorable to coöperative stores, and have allied themselves
with the Knights of Labor in several attempts at productive
coöperation. In Louisiana the Grange has organized a coöperative educational association, a school for their children.
With a modest capital of $8,000 an elementary school has
been started, paying dividends on the true Rochdale principle to stockholders and the public generally who patronize
the institution. In Georgia some little coöperation exists
among the farmers, who form clubs and purchase articles in
bulk and at wholesale rates. This is quite a common
method throughout the South. The Kentucky State Grange
had for many years a state agency in Louisville, but the

farmers fell into the hands of designing persons, who so manipulated their business that the agency got into the control of private parties. The cause of coöperation has been greatly weakened by this mishap, and a general distaste for its principles is manifest. However, " Church Hill " Grange, in Christian county, has pursued successfully the plan of dealing exclusively with one reliable house, which becomes their agent and grants them certain privileges. The one hundred and seventy members save by this process no less than $3,000 annually. The Kentucky Grangers have in their day had great political power, and by having railroad rates fixed by law at three cents per mile in the transportation of produce, have escaped many of the exactions that farmers' flesh is heir to. The Knights of Labor, also, have quite a successful store in Louisville, worked upon a coöperative plan. West Virginia has not been backward in distributive coöperation, and its true principles are being inculcated into youthful minds by the formation of classes among the farmers for the study of theoretical and practical coöperation. Maryland claims, however, the most successful agency in the order of Patrons, though its trade is not nearly as extensive as the Texas house. The agency was felt to be needed because of the high commission rates upon poor paying crops then demanded by merchants in Baltimore, and was started in 1876 with a cash capital of twelve dollars. Ten years of activity have increased the capital to over twenty thousand dollars. Started in a large city, without credit, and distrusted by many of the farmers, the agency has overcome many obstacles before attaining its present success. To facilitate business for the farmers in the western and northwestern portions of the state, the directors have established a branch agency in the city of Washington, granting it a portion of the capital of the state agency.[1] The gross busi-

----

[1] Gross business of Washington agency for 1887 amounted to $20,000.

ness and net profits of the state agency for a few years are
given in the accompanying table:

Year.	Total Business.	Net Profit.
1887	$290,859 76	$2,414 54
1886	319,845 73	6,219 13
1885	313,566 23	4,734 81
1884	362,485 76	3,584 55
1883		12,200 00
1882	547,501 13	3,801 75
1881		3,786 50

The profits are divided among the Patrons annually,
but are rarely withdrawn. By this means the capital of
the agency has been increased, and its business in consequence widely developed. A coöperative store is in operation at Rugby, Tenn., the community founded by Thomas
Hughes. The settlement was made in 1880 by a party of
colonists, conducted by Mr. Hughes in person, from England.
This ideal colony has flourished, though the ruling power is
in a London Board, with their agents at Rugby.[1] Very
contradictory reports are circulated regarding its present
and future, though there seems to be a unanimity of
opinion as to the greatness of its possibilities. The
Sovereigns of Industry, the great promoters of coöperation
in New England and the Middle States, had no existence
in the South, though the state of Maryland claimed a few
members in the early years of the organization. Yet the
influence of this order, as of the theories and principles of the
Patrons, are manifested in the zealous endeavors toward
coöperative enterprises witnessed in many parts of the South.
The Parkersburg Coöperative Association, incorporated
in July, 1885, is but one expression of this feeling. Parkersburg, W. Va., has among its citizens one of the most
zealous as well as energetic coöperators in the country,
M. P. Amiss, Esq., under whose direction this association
was founded, and by whom the principles of coöperation
were instilled by lectures to his brother citizens. The

---

[1] There are comparatively few coöperative features in this colony,
and no communistic features whatever.

association has a store which is reported as doing a good business, and contemplates the establishment of a coöperative canning factory this summer. The capital of the association is $10,000, divided into shares of ten dollars each. These may be purchased by installments, but no member can own more than five shares, or cast more than one vote. The profits are thus disposed of: "Two per cent. of profits shall form a contingent fund, or sinking fund, until a sum equal to thirty per cent. in excess of paid stock shall have accumulated; six per cent. shall be paid as interest on the capital stock; the remaining profit is to be divided among the members according to their purchases."

The Clinton Coöperative Company, of Baltimore, is achieving a success in coöperative distribution. The company was incorporated in May, 1887, with a capital of six hundred dollars. A grocery store is now in active operation, and is well patronized by the Knights of Labor. The shareholders number forty-three. These are allowed a credit up to six dollars; all others deal upon a strictly cash basis. Quarterly an account of stock is taken and a dividend declared, which by agreement is for the first year turned in to increase the capital. This dividend amounted to nineteen per cent. at the end of the last quarter.

III.

LOAN, AID AND BUILDING SOCIETIES.

Loan societies may lay true claim to priority over any other form of coöperation. The principle involved had its origin in the earlier days of pre-historic man, when one lent another his services in the construction of houses, in the tilling of fields, or in the care of flocks. In return he received like assistance, or some proportion of the produce of flocks or fields. Germinal types of the loan, of the beneficial and of the building societies are here seen, though the first attained no permanence before Christian principles leavened the race of men. During the early centuries of

Christianity, societies existed among its votaries whose
object was to aid the brethren in distress, and especially to
provide for their burial.   Such societies were authorized by
the Roman law, and received its sanction and protection.
Regular dues were paid to the "Collegium" by its members
who received in return a guarantee of burial.   By the inde-
fatigable labors of such societies the vast catacombs of Rome
were built, a wonder for later ages.   From that time to the
present the church and Christian precept have played an
important part in the organization of beneficial societies of
all sorts, rendering practical assistance as well as spiritual
encouragement.

Loan and building societies are much the same the
country over, differing merely in the character of members
and in success of operation.   In the South they had rare
existence before the war, a few isolated cases only being
found in the larger cities.   After 1865 they sprang up like
mushrooms, generally with little security of foundation and
loose in management.   The laws of the states made it easy
to start them, but took little care that they should be limited
strictly to a legitimate business.   Five individuals might
meet, contribute a few dollars each, and incorporate themselves as the Smithville Loan and Building Association.
They would in their corporate capacity issue their stock, and
returns would come in rapidly, with few loans at first to
exhaust the capital.   Here was a chance for peculation, which
was frequently attempted.   While the managers used the
capital, reserving a small sum for dividends, all looked well.
At last some stockholder desires to withdraw and applies
for his money.   Here came the rub.   With little cash on
hand the officers would give a note on the company, not
their own; other stockholders would become frightened; a
run is made upon the concern and the collapse comes.   The
association corporately pleads *"nulla bona,"* but the
managers individually have made enough to incite them to
start another loan and building association.   Owing to such
frequent failures among them during the ten years following

the war, more stringent laws were everywhere passed. An element of safety was introduced by making the president and officers personally responsible. But abuses and consequent failures continued so long as the societies could issue notes in lieu of dividends or shares. This was remedied in Maryland by an act of 1878, forbidding any such society "to issue any promissory note, bill or obligation of any kind to any member thereof, or borrow therefrom in lieu of money, and that all loans of such corporations shall be made in money and not otherwise." The societies now in existence, and there are many of them in Maryland, are upon a good footing and afford to a certain class of people inducements to borrow money and improve homesteads. Good real estate security, or something deemed equivalent, is required before the association will lend a cent. The loan is made as a rule to stockholders only, and the rate of interest is excessive. To wipe out his debt the borrower pays twenty-five cents weekly per one hundred dollars, and fifteen cents on the same as interest. For example, A. wishes to borrow five hundred dollars of a loan society of which he is not a member. He must buy at least one share, mortgage his house and lot, and then pay at the above rates over eight hundred dollars before he can redeem his mortgage and declare himself free from debt.[1] He is fined if he misses a weekly payment, is charged for the drawing of the mortgage, and, though his actual debt grows less weekly, he pays a high rate ever increasing until the debt is extinguished. The officers and stockholders who do not borrow regard themselves as philanthropists in a mild way, while a calm outsider recognizes such an institution as a fraudulent

---

[1] For one share of stock, say .... $ 5 00
To twenty-five-cent payments, 7 years 9 months 500 00
To fifteen-cent payments for same time 300 00
                                                          _____
                                                          $805 00

The borrower commences by paying at the rate of seven and eight-tenths per cent. interest, and is allowed no reduction on credits.

humbug that hides its misdeeds under the cloak of a good name.

The coöperation is here strictly confined to the non-borrowing stockholders. So numerous are these societies in Baltimore, especially among the Germans, that names fail them to style their associations, so they adopt the name of the street upon which the office is. Fortunately there are better forms of building and loan societies. Another method employed in the loaning of money is used by the Washington Coöperative Building Asssociation, of the District of Columbia. The association issues stock at a par value of one thousand dollars, and the shares are paid for at the rate of two dollars and a half a month. At the end of every month or fixed period a surplus has accumulated from such installments and from fines, and this is loaned to the members who bid the highest rate of interest. The bidder must own stock to the amount of his loan, though not paid for, and must give a sufficient mortgage security.

The mortgage being turned over to the company, the highest bidder receives his loan, payable in six years. The officers of the company are all bonded, and their business is very extensive. A stockholder is permitted to draw out when he chooses, receiving all he has put in and six per cent. interest thereon. The interest is rarely higher than eight per cent., and the borrower is never actually swindled, though the method of bidding may introduce a speculative feature.

Another method, still pursued by some of the loan societies and the Sovereigns of Industry in the Northern states, was the following: The association borrowed money from ndividuals, guaranteeing six per cent. interest. This is sub-loaned by the association at the rate of ten per cent. to the borrower who bids the shortest term. Thus the capital can be turned over often, and the margin of four per cent. pays all expenses of management. In the Southern states societies of this character have had a comparatively recent origin.

Among the slave populations the idea of associations for any purpose was contrary to the spirit of the law, and any attempts at such were vigorously stopped. Gradually, however, there grew up the free-black population of the South, composed of slaves voluntarily freed or of those who had purchased their freedom by years of toil. They were a better class, mentally and economically, than their brethren in slavery. The first idea of the freed slaves was to leave the plantation and flock to the towns and cities, and there to form secret societies. The element of secrecy was always most popular. As early as 1835 such societies of free-blacks existed in the cities of the South. Baltimore was the stronghold of their class, and their number was great here. Societies sprung up in city and country connected with their churches, but here, as in most of these societies, an officer of the law was required to be present at the meetings. The number of free-blacks increased largely in the decade immediately preceding the war, numbering in Maryland alone, in 1860, nearly eighty-four thousand; in Virginia fifty-four thousand. To some extent slaves were admitted to their societies, though this was forbidden by law, because it was supposed that such associations gave assistance to slaves to escape from bondage. There is and always has been to the colored people an indescribable charm in secret conclaves and symbols. So suspicious were their actions often in their meetings that not infrequently, before the war, the courts would authorize a raid upon their temple, and a strict scrutiny of their records by a court official. During the years of the war and those immediately following, negro beneficial societies exercised little influence, but from 1867 to the present their growth has been phenomenal. The first associations were either connected with churches or were masonic in character. The Odd Fellows were organized in Maryland as early as 1837, and claim an earlier and more direct descent from the English society than do their white brethren, having been formed under a charter brought out that year from the mother

country. The order of the Good Samaritans was, perhaps,
the next instituted, in 1841, and these two organizations
now number their membership by thousands in Maryland
alone.[1]

From Maryland these masonic societies spread over Virginia, Kentucky and Tennessee, admitting all ages and
both sexes into their various male, female and juvenile
departments. Few negroes in good standing in the cities
of the South belong to one society alone, and often a man,
active in such works, can claim a membership in six distinct
lodges or societies at the same time.

Beneficial societies lacking masonic mysteries have had
little popularity among the negroes, but, so far as learned,
have had excellent results. They are of two classes, on the
mutual benefit principle, with regular periodical dues, and
on the assessment principle, dues being dependent upon the
mortality of the members. The former, from its certainty,
is deservedly the more popular form. Take for example
the Maryland Mutual Benefit Association, incorporated in
February, 1885, as a sample of the first class. Members
pay weekly dues varying at choice from five to twenty-five
cents, and receive in turn, when sick, a weekly benefit
varying from seventy-five cents to seven dollars, and a
funeral benefit of from eight to fifty dollars. The membership of this particular society is small, yet it has eight
branch offices in different towns of the state, and has paid
out quite a sum in benefits within its three years of existence. Assessment societies are worked on a rather different
principle. As an example of this class we may take the St.

---

[1] The order of the Galilean Fisherman, another colored beneficial
society, originated in Baltimore, in 1856. Its organization is secret,
composed of men, women and children, and its membership is
26,000 in nine states, managed by 400 right worthy rulers, 400 secre-
taries and 1,200 committees on the sick. Over $25,000 has been
paid into its treasury, of which over $20,000 has been disbursed in
charities of some kind. Baltimore city's membership is about
2,700, divided among fifteen lodges.

33

James' Beneficial Society, organized about 1850 among the colored members of St. James' Church, Baltimore. The members pay a regular monthly fee of fifty cents, and receive a weekly benefit, in case of sickness, for eighteen months. Moreover, the brother members are required to act as nurses to the sick, and accomplish great good thereby. If the member becomes a chronic invalid he is supported upon a gradually diminishing allowance for two years. In case of a death the society guarantees thirty dollars in an immediate payment, and an additional amount raised by a levy of twenty-five cents on every member. The colored beneficial societies have been, as a rule, well managed, and few cases of insolvency are reported. Greater security from financial difficulties is insured in having a large committee do the work of the treasurer, and by a mutual distrust thus engendered, the possibilities of peculation are reduced to a minimum. Possibly harm is done in stimulating a desire for large and costly funerals, yet the good accomplished far outweighs this. If a member dies on Monday his body usually remains unburied until the following Sunday when the whole organization can turn out and parade. This desire for display is, however, inherent in negroes, and they follow the example of their more enlightened white brethren. The good that such societies have accomplished can not be questioned. During the war and immediately thereafter, negroes could be seen begging on every corner to heal their sick and bury their dead. This is a thing of the past, and the number of negro paupers buried by local authorities, city or county, or supported at public expense in alms-houses, has been wonderfully reduced in the past twenty years. There is an inherent horror in the heart of every negro of being cared for and buried by the public, doubtless increased by the dread of certain use after death for the cause of the medical science. Medical schools, in consequence, are so often reduced to extremities that they are driven to look for subjects in other than the Potter's fields. There are over a hundred colored societies in Mary-

land, and their membership is variously estimated at from
ten to fifteen thousand. Kentucky and Tennessee have
each nearly as many. Begun in the simpler forms, they
have in many instances expanded into literary, pension and
insurance societies, though they are very shy of the more
complex features.

Few loan or building societies exist among the negroes,
which may be explained in three ways: First, from the fact
that the colored people as a rule have little desire to acquire
property in the cities, where the societies exist, whereas in
the country districts this desire often amounts to an insanity.
Again, if they wish to purchase or improve property in
town, they prefer accumulating in the old stocking, or bor-
rowing on notes from banks. Their trust in banking institutions of all sorts is small, and has been greatly lessened
by the miserable failure and fraud connected with the late
Freedmen's Savings Bank.[1] A third cause is undoubtedly
in the feeling that they are themselves incapable of conduct-
ing a business of that character, and prefer to leave it to
their white brethren, who in most cases allow them equal
privileges. Thus in Charlestown numerous charters of
colored loan and building societies have been recorded but
not one as yet started. · Baltimore has but one building
society exclusively managed by negroes.

---

[1] The story of this institution is well known. Chartered by Congress, March 3, 1865, thereby receiving the sanction and approval
of the government, the Freedmen's Bank was an incentive to the
newly-created citizens of the South to save their first earnings. It
was founded, not to carry o ɪ a banking business, but its object "was
to receive deposits on behalf of persons heretofore held in slavery
in the United States, and of their descendants, and invest the same
in stocks, bonds, treasury notes, and other securities of the United
States." (Charter). In 1870 the managers without authority applied
for a change of charter allowing them to do a banking business with
the deposits. This was granted by Congress, and speculation, in
four years, caused the collapse and suspension of the bank (June
30th, 1874). The deposits on its books amounted to two million
dollars. Senator Call's bill, appropriating $1,200,000 to the
depositors and their representatives, has just become a law, but the
greatest difficulty is experienced in tracing the original depositors.

IV.

RAILROAD RELIEF ASSOCIATIONS.

Maryland is the centre and birth-place of one of the largest beneficial associations started in this country. Railroad relief and insurance associations had been in existence many years in England and the continent when the Baltimore and Ohio organized their system. Its origin was largely due to the lessons taught by the railroad riots in 1877, showing clearly the need of a more compact and coöperating system in the management of the road, and of a firmer bond of union between employer and employé.

Sixty per cent. of the employés were induced by the company's agents to petition for the establishment of a relief department in connection with the road, and acting upon this "petition" the Baltimore and Ohio Relief Association was inaugurated in May, 1880. The company clearly recognized the advantages accruing to them as well as to the employés in such a society. It was then regarded, and is still, as a purely business undertaking, savoring little of philanthropy. The company contributed the sum of $100,000 as a nucleus of the fund, and guaranteed certain privileges to the members of the association. Among these were free transportation on the road, under ten miles, for the children of contributors going to school, half fares for contributors and their families, and free medical attendance to those injured in the performance of duties. Participation was made compulsory for all employés and officers, except those receiving a salary of $2,000, or who were engaged in duties not deemed hazardous, or who failed to pass physical examination. Five classes of contingency were provided for; (1) to an employé disabled temporarily in the discharge of duty, a daily allowance for six months; (2) to the same in case of permanent disability, an allowance; (3) in case of death the payment of a stipulated sum to his representatives; (4) to the employé injured other than by accident in discharge of duties, an allowance for one year; (5) to the same in case of death, a specified sum. A regular scale of benefits and of monthly dues exists. Those receiving, thirty-five dollars or under pay one dollar monthly, and receive a daily benefit of twenty-five to fifty cents and a death benefit of·$100 to $500, depending upon the class of contingency. Dues and benefits are graduated up to those receiving one hundred dollars or over per month, paying a monthly contribution of five dollars, and receiving a sick benefit of one dollar and a-half per day and a death benefit of $2,500. These death benefits have been largely increased since their start without an increase in the contribution. As a precaution against the infirmities of old age a system of annuities was at the same time started, optional however, with employés. Contributions to this fund must be continued until the age of sixty-five, after which the contributor receives an annual allowance during life, equal to ten cents on every dollar contributed to the fund, and one-half cent for every year he has contributed. Example: A. contributes five dollars for thirty years, from the age of thirty-five to that of sixty-five. At the end of this period he will have $1,800 to his credit. His annuity will be one hundred and eighty dollars plus two dollars and seventy cents or one hundred and eighty-two dollars and seventy cents. In the event of death before the attainment of the age of sixty-five his representative receives the whole amount contributed and a sum equal to one-half this in addition. All members of the relief association must be under forty-five and have passed a physical examination at their entrance.

After two years of successful operation the Baltimore and Ohio Relief Association was incorporated by the General Assembly of Maryland, in 1882.

Seeing that the field of coöperative usefulness could well be enlarged, the following August (1882), supplementary organizations were added in a savings bank and building association for the benefit of the members of the relief association. Members are allowed to deposit from

one dollar to one hundred dollars per day at any railroad
station or office, and are guaranteed four per cent on such
deposits. Depositors are allowed a vote, for every twenty-
five dollars deposited, in the election of two trustees, the
railroad company selecting three. Surplus dividends may
be declared every three years.

The building association scheme is open to all members
of the relief association having fifty dollars on deposit in the
savings institution. Borrowers obtain money at six per
cent. interest on good security, and must repay at the rate
of one dollar per month on the hundred until the whole is
paid, each payment being deducted from the loan. Money
is loaned only for the purchase of homesteads or their improve-
ment, and the company allows great reduction in the transpor-
tation of building materials, and, when desired, the services
of an inspector. On the 14th of October, 1884, a new feature was introduced in the shape of a superannuation or
pension fund. It was endowed by the gift of $25,000 a year
from the railroad, and a payment of $100,000 to it from the
relief association. Pensioners must be members of the
association, and must have been ten years in the company's
employ. The fund is entirely supported by the donations
of the company, and no payments are made to it by individuals. The pension roll numbers one hundred and sixty-
five persons.

One can readily conjecture the scale of the association's
work, and the vast amount of good it has been doing over
the great system of the Baltimore and Ohio Railroad. With
headquarters in Baltimore, the membership of the association reaches from the Carolinas to New York, from Baltimore to Chicago. It now amounts to 22,155. The great
financial work that this association has built up, in its four
departments, may be seen from a glance at the accompanying table.

RELIEF ASSOCIATION.

	Receipts.	Disbursements.
May, 1880-January, 1881 (8 months).$	88,543 26	$ 41,503 14
Jan., 1881–Oct., 1882 (21 months) ...	345,088 30	302,617 69
October, 1882–1883..................	341,850 55	205,157 40
" 1883–1884..................	335,686 04	220,467 31
" 1884–1885..................	289,894 52	264,443 87
" 1885–1886..................		335,570 59
" 1886–1887..................	368,525 00	346,776 00
Total, 1880–1887...........	$.............	$1,716,536 00

SAVINGS FUND AND LOANS.

	Deposits.	Loans on Mortgages
August, 1882–October, 1883 ....$	82,555 35	$ 48,440 64
October, 1883–1884.....................	148,065 17	99,869 11
" 1884–1885.................	217,173 37	168,375 71

The executive officer of the relief association is the secretary. This position was first occupied by Dr. W. T. Barnard, under whose careful management the association took root. Dr. S. R. Barr is now secretary.

A sustained membership of 18,400 for five years, and the distribution of $1,716,536 in 67,560 payments among its members are facts sufficient in themselves to warrant the belief that the association is becoming an important feature in the Baltimore and Ohio system, productive of beneficent results. The employés have patronized with avidity the savings and loan features. The deposits of the former amount already to $273,132, of which $159,440 has been loaned for building and improving homes, and but twenty-six per cent. of this has been withdrawn since the bank opened.

The coöperative work of the railroad company has not stopped here. A free circulating library, liberally supported by the company, is in active and useful operation. An improved system of apprentices in the various departments, and a common school education in free night schools, at the expense of the company, contribute to the improvements of labor and the laboringmen.

Finally, the company has purchased a site for a sanitarium and home for its disabled and aged employés and their families, and now distributes medicines among them. There are disadvantages in such a relief association when viewed through other glasses than those of the railroad company. Even the utopian schemes evolved from philosophers' brains have always two sides; and so also must such a practical, worldly plan of a soulless corporation. In spite of the many admirable features the employé views it with distrust because it is an instrument by which the company gains a well-nigh absolute control over his fortunes and happiness. It is a tie that binds too tightly. The various features of the association are inextricably intertwined, and the compulsory feature is dominant. Moreover, membership in the association precludes the possibility of a suit for damages against the company, and an attempt at such forfeits the member's rights and interest. Yet, when a year or so ago the company solicited of its sixteen thousand employés their opinions upon the association and its workings, favorable replies came from every quarter save one, Chicago. Objection from this quarter is a chronic affection, and could not be treated with great respect. The relief system was based upon what was deemed best in various kindred associations in England, France and Germany, and, if not perfect, at least it shares the common misfortune of men and things.[1]

Following in the track of her greatest rival, the Pennsylvania Railroad Company on the first of February, 1886, instituted the Pennsylvania relief system. The company had watched closely the start and successful working of the Baltimore and Ohio system of relief, and introduced it at first as a compulsory feature among their employés.

They had boasted that their employés were in such perfect harmony with the administration, and already so identified

---

[1] See "The Relation of Railway Managers and Employès," by Dr. W. T. Barnard, and "The Labor Problem," by Prof. R. T. Ely.

with the road and its prosperity, that no subterfuges were to be resorted to in introducing the system. The result of many disputations, protests and strikes on the part of the coerced employés was the complete banishment of the compulsory feature. The Pennsylvania Railroad Voluntary Relief Department was now organized, and on the first of May, 1882, six of the railroads composing the vast Pennsylvania system entered into the plan. These were the Pennsylvania Railroad Company, the Northern Central, the West Jersey, the Philadelphia, Wilmington and Baltimore, the Camden and Atlantic, and the Baltimore and Potomac Railroad Companies. The administrative machinery consists of a manager or superintendent appointed by the company, assisted by an advisory committee of five, of which he is *ex officio* a member. The members of the Relief Department, or contributors, have each a vote and elect annually three of the advisory committee. The company undertakes to support the administration and meet all deficiencies. If any surplus remains in the Relief Department it is used for the promotion of a fund for superannuated members.

Membership dues are deducted monthly in advance from the wages to the credit of the contributor, in amount depending upon the class to which he belongs. These classes are five in number, based upon the amount of monthly wages, and the contributions vary from seventy-five cents to three dollars and seventy-five cents per month. The relief benefit is fifty cents per day for the lowest class for fifty-two weeks, and half that amount thereafter during disability. For the other classes it rises proportionately, reaching two dollars and fifty cents for the highest. If the disability or sickness is other than from accident in the company's service, the benefit is forty cents for the lowest, rising to two dollars for the highest class, continuing for fifty-two weeks. Death benefits vary from $250 to $1,250. This company, like the Baltimore and Ohio, pays for all necessary surgical attendance during disability. Moreover, like the other railroad relief system, the members forfeit all rights, interest and reliefs if they prosecute the company for damages. In spite of the opposition which characterized its birth, the Pennsylvania Railroad relief system has met with most gratifying results in its short life.

The total membership of the department December 31st, 1886, was 19,952, distributed as follows: Pennsylvania Railroad Division, 16,096; Philadelphia, Wilmington and Baltimore, 1,569; Northern Central Railroad, 1,595; Baltimore and Potomac Railroad, 290; West Jersey, 258; and Camden and Atlantic, 144.

The total income of the Relief Department from membership dues for 1886 was $260,954.90, and the total benefits paid for death, accident and sickness amounted to $151,147.87; for January, 1887 ,$23,187.20. A good deal of space has been given to the subject of railroad relief in this paper because of the great principle involved, applicable as well to every branch of industry, to every great undertaking of modern industrial life. The success of the systems in vogue in the two greatest railroads of the country will undoubtedly lead to its further extension in this and other corporate enterprises.[1]

A system of state insurance and relief, as practiced in Germany, will in all probability be a thing of the distant future. Until this time shall come the management of relief systems by corporations is a step in the right direction toward coöperative association, and will promote beyond question the friendly relations of labor and capital. They do not pose as philanthropic associations, but, in promoting the welfare of their own employés, they do a greater and nobler work than many of the so-called coöperative, beneficial institutions managed by the laboring classes themselves.[2]

---

[1] Compulsory beneficial associations are now forbidden in Maryland by an Act of 1888.

[2] The West Virginia Central Railroad has a relief department with a membership of four hundred and ninety. Receipts, 1887, $1,889.85. Disbursements, $880.59.

V.

PROFIT-SHARING.

Whenever a workman has it within his power to increase the quantity of his production, to improve its quality, or reduce the cost price, by efficiency in workmanship and increased economy, profit-sharing may be introduced effectively with a gain to capital and labor. Through the will and individual care of the workman a profit is realized. It is produced by the enhanced efficiency of labor and from it the laborer is to be remunerated. Skilled labor is the essential to a successful scheme of profit-sharing, where the capital invested in tools and material bears a small proportion of the cost of production, and where superintendence is both difficult and expensive. Where machinery plays the important part and labor is of an unskilled and unprogressive character, profit-sharing will gain no foothold. Capital is here all-important and the profits of the enterprise pay an interest on the money sunk in machinery while labor is unimportant and easily controlled.

In industrial partnership, as profit-sharing enterprises are frequently termed, labor and capital are brought into alliance, capital and greater skill in management are united with interested and progressive labor. This introduces us to an all-important factor which places profit-sharing far in advance of the average forms of coöperation. It is the indispensable *business* capacity, necessary for the success of any trade or profession, yet so generally wanting in the inexperienced and in those who rely upon their daily labor for their daily food. The management of a business which involves waiting and delays, buying and selling, above all a capital and credit, requires a guiding mind devoted to its interest and advancement, an industrial pilot who knows the existence of rock and sand-bar, and can guide his craft safely. This business head is the element which so many coöperative undertakings lack, and is their great obstacle to success.

The field for profit-sharing is as limited as it is new in the South, except in that questionable form of farming-on-shares, to be later treated.

The principle attempts at the system have been in coal and iron mines, and in iron foundries. Texas, Alabama and Georgia can furnish several instances in their newly developed mining industries. In Maryland there exists one notable case in the management of the Union Mining Company at Mt. Savage. Through the kindness of the president, Mr. James S. Mackie, I have obtained a minute account of this newly started experiment.

To anticipate and avoid a strike among their employés, strikes having occurred in neighboring mines, the company determined to inaugurate a profit-sharing system in their works. The proposition was made to the employés, and accepted, and the scheme went into active operation January 1st, 1886. The provisions of the agreement were, in brief, that the directors pledge themselves to pay to their employés, annually or semi-annually, an amount equal to ten per cent. on every dividend made to the shareholders; the said percentage to be pro-rated according to the earnings of each man on the pay-rolls for the time covered by the dividend. Salaried employés were excluded, from the fact that no interruptions from weather or lack of work curtailed their regular incomes. The company protected itself from any attempt of management on the part of the employés or oversight of the books. The company, moreover, could terminate the system at the close of any year. The division of profits is among the workmen in all the departments, miners, brickmakers, foundrymen, carpenters and laborers, and is made on the basis of the aggregate earnings of the whole system.

The first dividend was declared in July, 1886, payable on September 15th, and varied from sixty-seven cents to twenty-three dollars per capita, depending on the time of service. Universal gratification was expressed by the two hundred and fifteen participators, who had little faith in any considerable advantage to themselves from the scheme. Indeed, before the distribution occurred, offers were made to sell out their interests for seventy-five cents, but with no takers! The second dividend was made in March, 1887, when about $3,000 was divided among two hundred and fifty employés. Hardly had this been paid, when in April a large number of the employés struck, refusing the arbitration offered by the company. The profit-sharing system has for the present been discontinued and the good are suffering for the actions of•the obstinate and foolish. The Union Mining Company, through its care for the welfare of its employés, deservedly had for six years perfect exemption from the evil of strikes. Twenty years ago the company, on principle, discontinued its store and allowed it to be managed by private parties. It was later found that the store-keepers dealt almost exclusively in bills against the company, a system caused, perhaps, by monthly payments of wages. This was found so injurious in tendency that it was broken up in 1883 and the store introduced a cash basis, made easier by weekly payment of wages.¹ In May, 1884, the company donated a park for the use of, and under the control of its employés and their families. To further still their thrift and encourage cleanliness and taste in the management of their dwelling houses, Mr. Mackie has divided his tenements into five districts, and in each offers a prize of one month's rent, whatever it be, to the tenant who shows during the year the greatest improvement and taste.

Though a careful examination of such a large field is well-nigh impossible, I have found the existence of profit-sharing limited to a few kinds of undertakings in the South, and by far the most prevalent form is farming-on-shares.

---

¹Maryland Code of 1878, section 170, article 40. "No railroad or mining company......shall own, conduct, or carry on any store or have any interest in any store, or receive any portion of the profits thereof, etc.''

Farming-on-shares, viewéd economically, approaches nearer the principle of profit-sharing than any other form of coöperation. The capitalist is represented in the land-owner, the machinery in the land, and labor in the tenant. Though the law of increasing returns is not as applicable to farming as manufacturing, yet increased skill in the use of natural advantages and properties will net increased pro-duction or a cheapness in production. The métayer system has, however, met no mercy at the hands of English economists, who maintain that by this method the land is miserably cultivated, and the agricultural population reduced to poverty. These necessary consequences to such a universal custom have been met by Sismondi, who, as practical farmer as well as economist, has witnessed excel-lent results from the métayer system of farming-on-shares. However, we are not discussing the consequences of the introduction of a questionable system into the country, but tracing the spontaneous growth and development of the system in the Southern states. Farming in the South prior to the late war was a truly excellent example of extensive cultivation. The typical Southern gentlemen, even before the days of George Washington, were planters living in large, rambling mansions upon their extensive acres. The farmer proper was the overseer, under whose management the plantation was worked by slaves, and its products disposed of, whether the owner was at home or abroad, or summer-ing at the springs. Overseers were usually paid in kind, and little money was ever handled in the administration of plantation economy. Here began the sharing of profits, and it was further increased by the growth of the free-negro population, who cultivated on shares land given them on manumission or bought gradually by the savings of years. The war and its consequences have completely changed the condition of agriculture in the South. From the close of the great civil strife the large plantations have been under-going partition in consequence of the social and industrial changes in progress. Tenants, overseers and former slaves have parted the homes of the aristocratic planters among them, either owning or working on shares.

These classes now form the bulk of the farmers, a hundred proprietors in the place of one planter. Of the total gain in the number of farms in the country since 1870, as recorded in the census of 1880, amounting to 1,348,922, 712,998 have been added in the former slave states. The acreage of farm lands in the South Atlantic states increased but twelve and four-tenths per cent. in the above decade, while the increase in number reached seventy-two and three-tenths per cent. The center of this system of farming-on-shares is to be found in the former slave states, though, of course, it exists everywhere.

Of the four million farms of the United States in 1880, seventy-four per cent. were worked by their owners, eight per cent. by tenants paid in money, and eighteen per cent. by tenants farming on shares. The preponderance of these in the South is attested by the fact that but eight and ninety-five hundredths per cent. are found in the North Atlantic group, and twenty-four and five-tenths per cent. in the South Atlantic and Central groups.

In lands thus worked the owner gets his share, or rent, in kind amounting to one-half or as low as one-fifth of the entire crop, varying according to crop, custom and conditions in the lease.

Now as to the effect of this much condemned species of cultivation upon the productivity of the soil and the well-being of the cultivators, it can be satisfactorily shown, I think, that in both particulars farming on shares has been eminently successful in the South. Intensive farming has been substituted for extensive, though perhaps the cultivators are not as intelligent a class. During the slavery period the planters paid no attention to rotation of crops or fertilizing, and, as a rule, lost yearly as farmers, yet they became rich men through "an unearned increment," the increase in their slaves. These slaves now own over eight millions' worth of land in Georgia alone, and, when working on shares, have proved more regular in their payments of shares or rent than white tenants.

Occasionally one finds examples of a more perfect form of coöperation in farming among the colored people of the South. A company of them will associate together, purchase a piece of land, and work it by turns or coöperatively. Thus one such scheme near Savannah has prospered, where seventeen negroes bought a two hundred-acre farm, some managing this, while others make a living by fishing and oystering. The coöperators live continually upon the farm, though carrying on their different trades in connection with it.

INDEX.

.

www.ingramcontent.com/pod-product-compliance
Lightning Source LLC
Chambersburg PA
CBHW031757090426
42739CB00008B/1042